A souvenir guide

Beatrix Potter's Lake District
Cumbria

Vivienne Crow

National Trust

Inspirational Lakeland

Beatrix Potter's love affair with the Lake District started when she was 16, during the first of many family holidays there.

It was a passion that inspired her famous children's books and, thanks to her legacy to the National Trust, lives on today in the landscape, farming practices and conservation ethos of this most spectacular corner of England.

In 1882, the Potter family – barrister Rupert, his wife Helen and their children Bertram and Beatrix – broke with their tradition of spending summers in Scotland. The Perthshire mansion they'd stayed in for 11 years was no longer available, which prompted Rupert to seek a new holiday location for his Kensington-based family. He chose the Lake District. It was a decision that was to have a profound impact on both the world of children's literature and the conservation movement in England.

Right The unspoilt Newlands Valley was a source of inspiration for Beatrix Potter, as were many other picturesque spots in the Lake District

'I do not remember a time when I did not try to invent pictures and make for myself a fairyland amongst the wild flowers, the animals, fungi, mosses, woods and streams, all the thousand objects of the countryside; that pleasant, unchanging world of realism and romance, which in our northern clime is stiffened by hard weather, a tough ancestry, and the strength that comes from the hills.'

The budding artist

The first of the Potters' Lake District holidays was spent at Wray Castle, a mock-Gothic mansion on the western shore of Windermere. This beautiful landscape of sparkling lakes, rolling farmland and sumptuous woods, all backed by craggy mountain scenery, was rich fodder for an open and imaginative mind such as Beatrix's. It was also the place where she first met Hardwicke Rawnsley, the vicar of nearby Wray Church and a man who would have a lasting influence on her life.

By the time she celebrated her 16th birthday, Beatrix had already developed an interest in sketching. During this first Lakeland holiday, it was the natural world to which she was particularly drawn. Trees, fungi, flowers and farm animals were closely observed and reproduced on paper. Her pets too, many of whom accompanied the family on their long summer breaks, were her subjects: rabbits, mice, frogs, even a lizard she found in Devon.

Shy and awkward, not in the slightest bit interested in the social whirl of Victorian London, it was from long family trips to the Lake District that she drew her early inspiration and gradually discovered where her heart lay.

Wray Castle

Wray Castle was built in the 1840s by retired Liverpool surgeon James Dawson. He spent much of his wife's inheritance on the project. Less than three miles from Hawkshead, the castle is now owned by the National Trust and is open to the public.

Top Beatrix produced this study of flowers when she was just ten years old

A rabbit named Peter

'Peter'

Jan - 98

From 1885 to 1907, the Potters spent many of their long summer holidays in the Derwentwater area of the north Lakes. It was during this period that Beatrix began writing picture stories, in letter form, for young relatives and the children of her former governess. One of these illustrated a mischievous little rabbit named Peter.

The Tale of Peter Rabbit was published in 1902. Beatrix struggled to get a publisher interested in it at first and, after several rejections, had it printed privately. Finally, with the help of some gentle pushing from her friend Hardwicke Rawnsley, the publisher Frederick Warne took it on. Her most famous book, it has been translated into dozens of languages and has sold almost 50 million copies around the world, making it one of the best-selling works of fiction ever.

Above Beatrix's pet rabbit Peter was the inspiration for her most well-known character. She drew this portrait in 1898

Opposite Beatrix painted this watercolour of a hillside pathway in September 1915, when she was holidaying near Derwentwater

The 'little books' take shape

The Tale of Peter Rabbit was followed over the next few years by a total of 22 stories, including at least three inspired by family holidays at Lingholm and Fawe Park on the shores of Derwentwater: *The Tale of Squirrel Nutkin* (1903), *The Tale of Benjamin Bunny* (1904) and *The Tale of Mrs Tiggy-Winkle* (1905). The illustrations are clearly based on real locations – Beatrix made no secret of that.

Unchanged landscape

Thanks to the conservation movement of which Beatrix was part, many of those scenes have changed little in the intervening decades. Where there is any doubt, we have the writer's own sketchbook – kept during a holiday to the Derwentwater area in 1903. Writing to her publisher just before that trip, she said, 'I had better try to sketch this summer, as the stock of ideas for backgrounds is rather used up.' And sketch she did – clambering up fellsides and exploring woodland glades, gathering material as she went. Just before her return to London, she wrote to her publisher again: 'I think I have done every imaginable rabbit background, & miscellaneous sketches as well – about 70!'

'My brother and I were born in London because our father was a lawyer there. But our descent – our interests and our joy – was in the north country.'

Northern roots

There was a sense, in the Potters' choice of the Lake District as their favoured holiday home, of the family returning to their roots: both Helen's and Rupert's ancestors were originally from the north-west of England, their wealth having been built largely on the textile industry. This northern heritage later became a source of some pride for Beatrix.

On location

Wander the Derwentwater area with one of the relevant Beatrix Potter tales, and it's easy to spot the places that inspired her illustrations.

Mrs Tiggy-Winkle

Cat Bells, the little summit above the lake so loved by walkers, is the home of Mrs Tiggy-Winkle. A 'door in the hill' leads into the hedgehog's house, probably based on one of the old mine entrances that Beatrix came across on her explorations. Mrs Tiggy-Winkle's human friend Lucie, meanwhile, lives in the Newlands Valley, the tranquil dale to the west. Lucie was based on a real child: Lucie Carr, the daughter of the Newlands' vicar. As a toddler, Lucie would play with Beatrix's pet hedgehog whenever her parents came to tea at Lingholm.

The scenery in this area is typical of the north-western Lakes: steep-sided, often craggy fells and splendid ridges soaring above glacial valleys that are home to becks tumbling down from the mountains via tumultuous waterfalls. To the east are the imposing slopes of the massive bulk of Skiddaw. All of these scenes are reproduced with considerable skill in *The Tale of Mrs Tiggy-Winkle*, revealing Beatrix to be as much a landscape artist as an illustrator of children's books.

Above Watercolour sketch of the Newlands Valley

Left Beatrix based the background in this picture on the Newlands Valley

Benjamin Bunny

The setting for *The Tale of Benjamin Bunny* is more geographically confined: Benjamin and his famous cousin Peter enjoy an adventure in Mr McGregor's garden, based on Beatrix's sketches of Fawe Park. The grounds of this private house are not open to the public, but the gardens can be glimpsed from a footpath that leads from Nichol End to Hawes End.

As in *The Tale of Squirrel Nutkin*, many of the woodland scenes are based on sketches that Beatrix drew while investigating the tree-covered shores of Derwentwater. Public footpaths enable visitors to wander these shores today, in and out of woods where the branches of grand old oaks tickle the water's edge. Many of the woods are privately owned, but some are in the care of the National Trust.

Squirrel Nutkin

In *The Tale of Squirrel Nutkin*, the squirrels are pictured paddling across to Owl Island to visit Old Brown, the owl. The wooded island, right out in the middle of the lake, is clearly St Herbert's Island, with Walla Crag and Falcon Crag forming a dramatic backdrop when viewed from near the Potters' holiday homes on the western side of Derwentwater.

Named after the long-time friend and disciple of St Cuthbert who lived the life of a hermit here in the seventh century, this secluded spot can be reached today in much the same way as Nutkin and his friends reached it: by paddling or rowing. But whereas the squirrels 'made little rafts out of twigs', humans are better off hiring a rowing boat or canoe from Keswick or Portinscale.

Above, left The squirrels on their rafts in *The Tale of Squirrel Nutkin*

Right The bunnies watch as Mr McGregor disappears into his house in *The Tale of the Flopsy Bunnies*

'East, south and north, the blue mountains with their crimson crests towered up against a clear blue heaven, flecked with little white fleecy clouds.'

Beatrix the businesswoman

Throughout her 20s and 30s, Beatrix Potter sought an independent income, and showed herself to be capable of doing so. 'It is something to have a little money to spend on books and to look forward to being independent,' she wrote in her journal in 1895.

Her first private earnings had come from the sale, a few years earlier – at the age of 24 – of six greeting card designs based on her pet rabbit, Benjamin Bouncer. Then, after the publication of *The Tale of Peter Rabbit*, she had a Peter Rabbit doll patented, the first of several moves towards merchandising.

Paying close attention to her publishing contracts and copyright issues, she revealed herself to be more than just a writer and illustrator; she was a businesswoman too. It was a trait that was to come in handy when she later used her royalties to buy property throughout the Lake District and run her own farms.

A bright and happy NEW YEAR.

Above One of Beatrix's very first greeting cards, published by Hildesheimer and Faulkner

Birth of the National Trust

The Potters' Derwentwater holiday homes were just a stone's throw from Brandelhow, the first Lakeland property bought by the National Trust. Hardwicke Rawnsley, an inspirational speaker, led the campaign to raise funds for its purchase after it went up for sale. The scheme received nationwide support, and Princess Louise, daughter of Queen Victoria and a supporter of the National Trust's work, performed Brandelhow's opening ceremony in October 1902.

Left This Grimwade tea set from the 1910s is displayed in one of the rooms at Hill Top (see page 12)

Above Peter Rabbit calendar, 1920

The 'perfect' place

The Potters didn't take their holidays exclusively at Derwentwater; they also spent several summers on the shores of Esthwaite Water, in Near Sawrey, in the south Lakes. Their first trip to the area that was later to become Beatrix's home was in 1896, and it was a holiday that left its mark on the 30-year-old.

'I think one of my pleasantest memories of Esthwaite is sitting on Oatmeal Crag on a Sunday afternoon, where there is a sort of table of rock with a dip, with the lane and fields and oak copse like in a trough below my feet, and all the little tiny fungus people singing and bobbing and dancing in the grass and under the leaves all down below, like the whistling that some people cannot hear of stray mice and bats, and I sitting up above and knowing something about them.'

Writing in her journal after returning to London in November 1896, she said: 'I was very sorry to come away in spite of the broken weather. It is as nearly perfect a little place as I ever lived in, and such nice old-fashioned people in the village.' She resolved to own a corner of this 'perfect' place one day, a dream she would fulfil before too long.

A fairy land

The area around Esthwaite Water fired Beatrix's imagination. The family stayed at a large house called Lakefield, later renamed Eeswyke, with wonderful views across the tranquil lake to the craggy Coniston mountains. She went on long walks with her brother, toured the district in pony and trap, and spent much time drawing and painting. The woods, in particular, filled her with 'childish fancies of wolves'. She thought they would make 'a very striking background ... for Grimm's Fairy Tales'. The lake eventually became the setting for her 1906 book, *The Tale of Mr Jeremy Fisher*.

Beatrix the mycologist

The rolling hills and woodland also proved a good place for her to learn more about fungi. She'd first developed a fascination for mushrooms and toadstools – as well as mosses and lichens – during holidays in the Highlands.

She was painstaking about her studies: sketching her subjects in beautiful detail and with scientific accuracy, growing specimens at home, and even preparing an academic paper on the subject. Although she wasn't taken seriously at the time – partly because of her gender – experts now agree many of her findings were correct. Today, some of her botanical sketches and a collection of watercolours can be seen in the Armitt Museum in Ambleside. They also form the basis of many delightful scenes in her 'little' books.

Opposite Esthwaite Water at dawn

Above Beatrix painted this view of Esthwaite Water and the hills and mountains beyond in 1905

Left Fungi study by Beatrix, 1893

Hill Top and Near Sawrey

As sales of her books grew, Beatrix's dreams both of financial independence from her parents and of owning a little corner of her Lake District paradise started to take shape. She used her royalties to buy her first property in 1903: a field near Esthwaite Water. Then, in 1905, she purchased Hill Top, the small farm in Near Sawrey that, since her death, has become a site of pilgrimage for Beatrix Potter fans from around the world.

Although still living with her parents in London, Beatrix made regular trips to her Sawrey properties over the next eight years, supervising building work, tending the gardens and learning about farming. In 1909, she bought Castle Farm, situated over the road from Hill Top.

The books keep coming

This was one of her most fruitful periods as a writer, and, delighting in her surroundings and her new role as a member of the local community, she set at least seven of her books in and around Near Sawrey.

The Tale of Jemima Puddle-Duck (1908) is just one of these, featuring pictures of her own Hill Top farmyard as well as the wife and children of her farm manager, John Cannon. Pigling Bland, Ginger and Pickles, Samuel Whiskers, Mr Tod and Tom Kitten are some of the other famous inhabitants of Beatrix's alternative Sawrey landscape.

Stories from her new life feature too: *The Tale of Samuel Whiskers* recalls a rat infestation at Hill Top. 'Mrs Cannon has seen a rat sitting up eating its dinner under the kitchen table in the middle of the afternoon,' she wrote to a friend soon after buying the farm.

Troutbeck Park

Beatrix didn't confine her property purchases to the Sawrey area: she bought up land, farms and cottages all over the central Lake District, eventually leaving them to the National Trust in her will.

Troutbeck Park in the heart of the eastern fells, bought in 1923, is one of the largest. It provides much of the inspiration for her 1929 book, *The Fairy Caravan*. Quite different to her early books, this story focuses on the things that had become so important to her in later life: Lakeland traditions, farming practices, even the hardy local sheep breed, the Herdwick.

In the preface to the book, published only in the USA during her lifetime, she wrote: 'Through many changing seasons these tales have walked and talked with me. They were not meant for printing: I have left them in the homely idiom of our old north country speech. I send them on the insistence of friends beyond the sea.'

Opposite **Hill Top**

Conservation in Lakeland

Throughout the late 19th and early 20th centuries, there was a growing desire to protect the Lake counties from development and to preserve its serenity.

Beatrix Potter entered this world at a time when the movement was gathering pace. With her passion for the natural world and her friendship with Canon Hardwicke Rawnsley, her involvement was almost inevitable.

An influential friendship

It was during the Potters' trip to Wray Castle in 1882 that Beatrix first met Hardwicke Rawnsley. He was the vicar of nearby Wray Church (later given the parish of Crosthwaite, near Keswick, and then made an honorary canon of Carlisle Cathedral) – and became a close family friend.

Recognising and nurturing her talent, he admired her artwork and showed an interest in her botanical leanings. He shared with her his enthusiasm for the landscape, for archaeology, geology and for farming, all the while inadvertently cultivating a fervent and loyal admirer. She couldn't help but be moved by this bold and ardent thinker, a man far removed from the relatively tame confines of her family life.

Lake District Defence Society

A highly educated individual, impassioned speaker and energetic campaigner, Hardwicke Rawnsley had already led a successful fight against building a mineral railway linking the Honister slate mine with Keswick via the pristine woods and lakeshore of Borrowdale. This campaign brought him to national prominence, a cartoon in the satirical magazine *Punch* depicting him as a knight saving the 'Ladies of the Lakes'.

Encouraged by this victory, he set up the Lake District Defence Society in 1883, the forerunner of the National Trust. Its aim was to prevent 'injurious encroachments upon the scenery ... from purely commercial or speculative motives'.

'It is most unfortunate how much has been wilfully destroyed in the English countryside. I have tried to do my humble bit of preservation in this district ...'

Footpath defender

One of Hardwicke's most noticeable triumphs came after landowners closed footpaths beside Derwentwater and over Latrigg, a small fell and popular viewpoint just north of Keswick. Hardwicke wrote letters of complaint, held protest meetings throughout the country and encouraged the ripping down of barriers across the paths. He was instrumental in gathering 2,000 people to march to the top of Latrigg, all singing 'Rule, Britannia!' at the top of their voices – a precursor of the 1932 mass trespass on Kinder Scout in the Peak District. The protesters eventually had their day in court – and won.

Opposite Canon Hardwicke Rawnsley

Left Hardwicke Rawnsley in the Lake District, 24 August 1904

Above Hardwicke Rawnsley (far right) with friends in the Lake District, c.1900

Preservation by acquisition

Beatrix shared Hardwicke Rawnsley's views on the need to protect not only the landscape and vernacular architecture, but also the unique character of Lakeland's rural traditions. It was he who established the first body looking after the interests of farmers of Herdwick sheep, the breed that she put so much energy into during her farming career.

Fearfully aware of large-scale, often unsympathetic development that was already taking place in the Lakes, Beatrix also shared his belief that the best way of going about conservation was through land purchase. This was the premise on which the National Trust was built and the principle that lay behind so many of her own acquisitions: land purchase not for ownership's sake, but to protect the land for the good of the entire nation in perpetuity.

Writing to Hardwicke's widow Eleanor long after his death in 1920, she emphasised this firm belief, saying, 'The Canon's original aim for complete preservation of as much property as possible by acquisition was the right one for the Lake District.'

'There is much talk in the Lake district about roads, building, rural planning and "amenity". It is well that public opinion is being roused at last ... This little corner of the country should be kept unchanged for people who appreciate its beauty.'

A movement builds

The idea of the Lake District belonging to the nation was first championed by the poet William Wordsworth (above, left), who was born in Cockermouth in 1770. In his 1822 *Guide to the Lakes*, he bemoaned modern threats to the landscape and the demise of local traditions. He described the Lakes as 'a sort of national property, in which every man has a right and interest, who has an eye to perceive and a heart to enjoy'.

Later in the century, the radical thinker John Ruskin (above, centre), who made his home at Brantwood on the shores of Coniston Water, took up the call. As a member, with Hardwicke Rawnsley, of the Thirlmere Defence Association, he fought against the construction of Thirlmere reservoir, though this battle was lost. At a national level, he promoted the importance of planning regulations, green belts and smokeless zones.

Hardwicke had been an earnest student of Ruskin's at Balliol College, Oxford, and kept in touch with his mentor in the Lake District. Another of the National Trust's founders, Octavia Hill (above, right), was also heavily influenced by Ruskin's thinking, and during the 1860s he invested in her social housing schemes to help London's poor.

Left Sheep grazing in the Newlands Valley

A Move Towards Farming

There was never a clear-cut transition in Beatrix Potter's life from writing to farming. The 'little books' kept coming for a few more years, but, from the moment she purchased Hill Top, her interests and priorities slowly began to change.

Hill Top

Even after buying her first farm, Beatrix continued to live in Kensington. She hadn't yet broken away from her childhood home, and her parents had certain expectations of her: like all 'good' Victorian spinster daughters, she was expected to stay at home and look after her parents in their old age. But this dull life was never going to be enough for Beatrix.

As well as continuing to join in with the tradition of regular family holidays in the Lake District, Beatrix, now approaching her forties, would rush up and down from London by herself at every possible opportunity.

Extending the house

She was overseeing building work – having a new wing added to Hill Top in 1906, which would allow her farm manager John Cannon to continue living there with his family while she occupied the older part of the house. The extension was based on her own designs, sensitively drawn up to ensure the farm retained the architectural characteristics of that part of the Lake District.

Left The path leading to the front door at Hill Top is edged by a long border filled with cottage garden favourites

She was very hands-on, always keeping a close eye on tradesmen. In a letter to a friend, Beatrix wrote: 'I had rather a row with the plumber – or perhaps I ought to say I lost my temper! ... if he won't take orders from a lady I may pack him off & get one from Kendal.'

On one occasion, she narrowly escaped serious injury after falling through an upstairs floor. 'I don't think I ran any risk,' she later wrote, '... the rafters were too near together to permit my slipping through. The joiner & plasterer were much alarmed & hauled me out. I was very much amused.'

Gardens

With the help of her new neighbours, she was also attempting to lay out a garden – a garden that remains one of the highlights of a visit to Hill Top today. 'I am being inundated with offers of plants!' she wrote. 'It is very kind of people; and as it is the right time to thin & replant, I don't feel such a robber of the village gardens.'

Farm apprentice

During her frequent trips to the Lake District, Beatrix was steadily learning about farming – undoubtedly a challenge for this city-born woman. Buying stock, purchasing more fields to consolidate her holdings, and maintaining her property took up her time and energy. So did more mundane tasks such as bee-keeping, rodent control and ensuring she received her fair share of the manure that the county council swept from the roads.

Cash flow

An astute businesswoman, she never lost sight of the importance of the royalties from her 'little' books for her new farming enterprise. Although the flow of books produced gradually slowed down, she continued writing. In correspondence with her publisher Harold Warne in 1908, requesting a royalties cheque, she wrote: 'The farm is doing very well, but he [John Cannon] has gone & spent all the pig money in buying sheep. I should be glad of another bit of money presently. I have now got 10 cows, and 31 sheep.'

William Heelis

In all her local business transactions, Beatrix used a firm of solicitors based in nearby Hawkshead: W H Heelis & Son. The partner specialising in property was William Heelis, and he dealt directly with Beatrix. Not only did he offer advice, he attended land auctions on her behalf and could be counted on to oversee work on her properties while she was away. Slowly, but surely, they got to know each other until, in 1912, he proposed to her.

This wasn't Beatrix's first offer of marriage: her publisher Norman Warne had died within months of her accepting his proposal in 1905. That first betrothal met with her parents' disapproval, as did the second one – partly because they felt a country solicitor wasn't a good enough match for their daughter, but also because they had come to rely on her in their old age. But, despite their objections, Beatrix married William Heelis on 15 October 1913. Finally, she had a reason for escaping London on a permanent basis.

Opposite Herdwick sheep are a familiar sight in the Lake District thanks to Beatrix Potter (see page 28)

Left The farmhouse at Hill Top

Hawkshead and the Beatrix Potter Gallery

The offices of W H Heelis & Son were located in a 17th-century house in the middle of Hawkshead, a busy little market town just two miles north of Near Sawrey. Hawkshead today looks similar to when Beatrix first stepped into the offices in the early years of the 20th century – a charming higgledy-piggledy jumble of alleyways and timber-framed buildings overhanging cobbled lanes. The solicitors' office, left to the National Trust by William Heelis in 1945, is now home to the Beatrix Potter Gallery, housing exhibitions of her original drawings and watercolours.

Meet Mrs Heelis

From the moment Beatrix married William, the changes that had slowly been transforming her life over the previous few years took on a more permanent state. The Lake District became her sole home and much of her time was given over to farming.

Priorities change

Having had 18 works published between 1902 and 1913, Beatrix's two-books-a-year days were over. Aside from a collection of nursery rhymes produced earlier in her career but not published until 1917, her next book didn't come out until 1918. This was *The Tale of Johnny Town-Mouse*. Another book of rhymes, largely gathered from earlier work, followed in 1922. A gap of seven years then followed before her next work, *The Fairy Caravan*, was published – and this only in America.

Family commitments

Her father Rupert died in 1914 following a long illness – a period that saw her rushing up and down to London on a regular basis. Soon after, her demanding mother Helen moved permanently to Lindeth Howe (now run as a hotel) on the shores of Windermere.

War encroaches

On the farming front too, with the First World War taking labourers from the English countryside to the horrors of the trenches, Beatrix faced challenges. 'The ploughman has got his calling up, in the very middle of ploughing. I'm afraid I am not in a particularly good temper.'

Above Castle Cottage, where Beatrix lived with her husband William, is located over the road from Hill Top. It is not open to the public

Right Beatrix and William in 1913, the year of their marriage

'Somehow when one is up to the eyes in work with real live animals it makes one despise paper-book animals ...'

Married life

At the same time, Beatrix was settling into life as a married woman. She was again overseeing building work, this time to enable her and William to live in Castle Cottage – a short stroll from her beloved Hill Top. She also bought neighbouring land, extending the farm's boundaries. Among the acquisitions was Moss Eccles Tarn which she stocked with trout. The tranquil body of water, still a popular beauty spot, became a place for the couple to retreat to on summer evenings. 'Mr Heelis & I fished (at least I rowed!) till darkness ... it was lovely on the tarn, not a breath of wind & no midges.'

Under pressure to keep her publisher Frederick Warne & Co afloat following Harold Warne's imprisonment for fraud, she wrote to his brother Fruing in 1920, saying: 'I think it is only honest to tell you that the book is not getting on yet. The country is looking beautiful enough to give me inspiration; but I seem as if I can't screw it out, and my eyes are always tired.'

Troutbeck Park Farm

A major turning point in Beatrix's farming career was her purchase, in 1923, of one of the largest farms in the Lake District – Troutbeck Park. Totalling 760 hectares (1,875 acres) when she bought it, the property, situated a few miles north of Windermere, lies in what was then Westmorland.

The farmhouse itself squats at the base of Troutbeck Tongue, a slither of moderately high ground cradled by much loftier, altogether more serious neighbours that reach a high point of 784m at Thornthwaite Beacon. Even today, it remains an expanse of wild, lonely country, visited only by shepherds and the occasional walker in search of solitude.

Beatrix first visited the area in 1895 – during a family holiday to the Lake District. She described it as a 'lonely wilderness' and wrote: 'Troutbeck Tongue is uncanny; a place of silences and whispering echoes. It is a mighty table-land between two streams. They rise together, north of the Tongue, in one maze of bogs and pools. They flow on either hand ... and re-unite beneath the southern crags, making the table-land almost an island haunted by the sounds that creep on running waters that encompass it.'

Threat

When she heard developers were planning to build new homes on the valley floor, she stepped in, paying £8,000 to protect this magical place from what she saw as potential desecration, and safeguard the future of its sizeable flock of native Herdwick sheep. As she'd done at Hill Top, she consolidated her property over the next few years by buying up neighbouring parcels of land, even small farms, at every opportunity.

The farm was in a poor state when she bought it, and there was little she could do to improve it while the sitting tenants remained there. But, three years later, as soon as their agreement ended, she took over the management herself; she wanted a 'free hand' to make improvements before finding a new tenant. She had very firm ideas about what she wanted to do, and, having decided to bequeath Troutbeck Park to the National Trust, she even wrote to the charity's secretary, Samuel Hamer, giving detailed instructions on what the Trust should do with it 'if I should happen to end while the farm is still in my hands'. She knew her own mind – and she made sure other people did too.

'In the calm spacious days that seem so long ago, I loved to wander on the Troutbeck fell. Sometimes I had with me an old sheep dog, "Nip" or "Fly"; more often I went alone. But never lonely. There was company of gentle sheep, and wild flowers and singing waters. I listened to the voices of the little folk.'

Above Troutbeck Park is one of the largest sheep farms in the Lake District

Right This unfinished sketch by Beatrix may be of Troutbeck, date unknown

Teamwork

It's clear from the way Beatrix dealt with Troutbeck Park that she'd learnt a great deal about farming since her purchase of Hill Top back in 1905. She now had nearly 20 years' experience.

She knew it to be 'a most lovely place and a fine farm', but realised the streams were polluted, the drains blocked and the buildings virtually derelict. She also knew she needed local expertise to turn things around – the skills that come, not from just 20 years of farming, but from a lifetime of husbandry.

Tom Storey

With the previous owners gone, she appointed a farm manager, Jimmy Hislop, and a shepherd, Tom Storey, whom she enticed from a nearby farm with the promise of doubling his wages. Tom proved to be well worth the money, immediately suggesting a new treatment for liver fluke and quickly turning the farm's fortunes around. Before long, Beatrix asked him to manage Hill Top for her, and help her breed Herdwick sheep for showing. It was the start of a long and fruitful partnership.

Joseph Moscrop

Every spring, she also employed another skilled shepherd: Joseph Moscrop. For the rest of Beatrix's life, he would travel down from his home close to the Scottish border to help with lambing and, later in the season, shearing. She valued his opinion and, maintaining a steady correspondence, turned to him in times of trouble on the farms. 'It is always a pleasure to see the swallows again and Joseph's smile,' she wrote to him in March 1942, anticipating his lambing visit.

Above Beatrix with her beloved sheepdog Kep in the garden at Hill Top, c.1913

Opposite Beatrix's love of sheepdogs is apparent in these closely observed sketches and illustrations

Sheepdogs

From the moment she purchased Hill Top, Beatrix took an interest in the border collies used as sheepdogs. They were working dogs first and foremost, but she usually had a favourite that would become more of a pet. Hill Top's Kep was her first, and he was followed by Fleet, Nip and Fly among others.

In a 1987 newspaper interview, Anthony Benson, her Troutbeck shepherd from 1927, recalled his employer's softness towards her dogs. 'When the farm dogs reached a good age and were no longer able to work they were all pensioned off and she had a proper kennel built for them. And every time she visited Troutbeck Park that would be the first place she would go to – them old dogs. Some folks has them put down, but no she would keep them. There were 14 dogs there at one time.'

Herdwick Sheep

Herdwick sheep are as much a part of the Lakeland landscape as the white-washed cottages dotting the valley bottoms and the dry-stone walls snaking their way up the fellsides, so it was almost inevitable that Beatrix would take an interest in them.

Take a walk on the fells or, at lambing time, through the valleys, and you'll see Herdwicks. The ewes are grey, their lambs jet black, and they seem always to have a mischievous grin on their faces. They've been grazing the open fells for centuries – nobody really knows for how long, although there are many colourful theories to explain their origins, including a rather unlikely story that they came ashore from a Spanish Armada shipwreck.

They are among the hardiest of British sheep breeds, able to survive on the poorest land and in the toughest conditions. Their wiry fleeces keep out the worst of the weather: come wind, rain, snow or drought, most flocks stay on the tops all year round, brought down only for lambing, dipping, shearing, showing and tupping. In dire circumstances – when buried for days on end in snow-drifts, for example – they have been known to survive by eating their own fleeces.

Unique instinct

The fells consist mostly of common land on which farmers have grazing rights. The sheep from different holdings are not walled or fenced in; they are free to wander, but instinctively keep to their own area – or heaf.

Hard life for sheep and shepherd

Even when Beatrix bought her first farm at the start of the 20th century, the Herdwick was under threat. Its lambing rate is not as high as other breeds; a slow maturer, its meat is not ready to eat until it is at least a year or two old; and its rough wool has not always been popular.

Above Herdwick sheep near Stonethwaite, Borrowdale

Left Herdwicks are a very hardy breed of sheep

Hardwicke Rawnsley recognised these drawbacks and the threat posed by more productive breeds, but he also realised the Herdwicks' unique qualities were ideal for the Lakeland environment. In 1899, he set up the Herdwick Sheep Association, the forerunner of the Herdwick Sheep Breeders' Association (HSBA), which continues to promote the breed today.

'Our members sustain and uphold the cultural traditions of the Lake District that have made it the most loved of English landscapes. Because of the importance of our cultural tradition to this landscape we believe that it needs to be better understood, respected and supported. Without hill farmers, the cultural landscape is a body without a beating heart.'

Beliefs put into practice

Always influenced by Hardwicke Rawnsley's concerns and beliefs, it's no surprise Beatrix took up the baton of defender of the breed after his death in 1920. With Tom Storey, she built up a celebrated flock, repeatedly winning major prizes when farmers gathered at the local agricultural shows to parade their stock. Keswick, Loweswater, Ennerdale, Ambleside, Hawkshead, Eskdale: she won at all these shows and more. Tom described her as being 'as proud as a dog with two tails' when she first won a top prize in 1927.

Acceptance?

A few of her fellow hill farmers claimed she knew little about sheep and relied solely on Tom's guidance. But that didn't stop them asking her to judge at shows – praise indeed in the farming world – and, in 1943, electing her president of the Herdwick Sheep Breeders' Association. Although she died before taking up the position, the vote of confidence – having her hard work recognised by her peers – no doubt brought her immense pride and satisfaction.

In 2015, Amanda Carson, secretary of the HSBA, had this to say about Beatrix: 'She was passionate about the Herdwick sheep and recognised their importance in the landscape and the rural community... Mrs Heelis recognised the issues affecting fell farming including afforestation, liver fluke and low incomes and wrote many letters trying to raise awareness of the difficulties faced by fell farmers ... She was a marvellous woman of her time, intelligent and gifted and with an amazing foresight and understanding of farming in the Lake District.'

Legacy

When Beatrix left her farms to the National Trust, she also left strict instructions about maintaining the numbers of pure Herdwicks on some of those properties. Ever since, the Trust and its tenants have maintained those flocks, helping the breed to survive into the 21st century.

On the up

Recent years have seen something of a revival in the Herdwick's fortunes. Following its highly publicised threatened demise during the 2001 foot-and-mouth outbreak, clever marketing initiatives and the award, in 2012, of Protected Designation of Origin status to Herdwick meat, have done much to promote awareness of the breed and its associated products.

Local dialect

The word Herdwick probably comes from the old Norse *herd-vik*, meaning sheep pasture. (Norsemen began to settle in the Lake District in the 9th century.) A survivor of even earlier times can be seen in the sheep counting system, thought to derive from a Celtic language. Although the words differ slightly from one dale to the next, the numbers one to three are usually something like this: *yan, tyan, tethera.*

Opposite Archive photograph of a herd of Herdwicks in Little Langdale. Beatrix Potter helped the breed to survive into the 21st century

Left The farmer at Yew Tree Farm, Coniston, with his flock of Herdwicks

Lakeland Resident

Beatrix's life in the Lake District didn't revolve solely around farming and conservation; she also played an active role in the local community.

She joined various organisations, championed local causes and, through her involvement with the Girl Guides movement (see page 34), encouraged the next generation in their appreciation of the countryside.

Community
Describing her life in Near Sawrey in 1916, Beatrix wrote, 'I don't go out much, haven't time; and the little town seems nothing but gossip and cards .' From this, you could be forgiven for thinking that she hid herself away, focusing on farming and her role as wife to William, but nothing could be further from the truth. Although she wasn't interested in 'gossip and cards', she did take an active interest in the quality of life in the 'little town' of Hawkshead and its surroundings.

Landowners and tourists
She was elected to the Landowners' Community Association, a body which, among other things, ensured local roads and property boundaries were maintained. She was also involved with the Footpath Association, a campaigning group championed by her friend Hardwicke Rawnsley. Unlike many landowners at the time, she had an enlightened view of tourists having access to the countryside. She knew them to be 'perfect terrors' in leaving gates open or damaging walls – allowing livestock to wander – but she talked of it being 'a pity to hear of visitors being turned back from fell land'. This forward-thinking attitude to tourism and how it could help generate funds to further the cause of

Above For this illustration from *The Pie and the Patty-Pan*, and the others on the page, Beatrix may have taken her inspiration from the buildings and activities in Hawkshead

Left Illustration from *The Tale of Johnny Town-Mouse*

Opposite The Misses Pussy-cats in *The Fairy Caravan*

as outbreaks of measles among local children, and recognised the need for professional nursing care. Thanks to donations and fundraising activities, the group, with Beatrix as treasurer, was soon able to appoint the area's first district nurse.

She was concerned with health at a national level too: throughout the 1920s and 1930s, she supported the Invalid Children's Aid Association, using the much loved figure of Peter Rabbit to raise money for hospital beds for sick youngsters. Those helping the Peter Rabbit Fund, as it became known, received letters and illustrated cards that Beatrix regularly produced for the charity between 1925 and 1941.

preservation was illustrated in her later involvement with Yew Tree Farm, part of the Monk Coniston estate, where she turned a parlour into a summer tearoom and worked hard to encourage visitors.

Public health

In 1919, long before the days of the National Health Service, Beatrix helped establish the Hawkshead District Nurse Association. She'd witnessed the flu epidemic that raged across Europe at the end of the First World War as well

The next generation

Another group that kept Beatrix busy – and provided her with many moments of pleasure – were the Girl Guides. Some commentators take great pleasure today in depicting the writer and illustrator of children's book as someone who despised youngsters. Indeed, she is on record as describing the 'modern child' as 'pampered & spoilt with too many toys & books'. But she was always happy to welcome well-behaved Girl Guides to camp on her land and learn about the countryside she so adored.

'It is always a pleasure to help Guides, and it brings its own reward – for surely it is a blessing when old age is coming, to be able still to understand and share the joy of life that is being lived by the young. If I slept in a tent I might get sciatica; I enjoy watching Guides, smiling in the rain.'

Left Beatrix Potter poses in a Girl Guides campsite, c.1930

Above Beatrix Potter
with a group of girl
guides, c.1940

Hydroplanes on Windermere

In 1912, Beatrix became involved in a battle to stop the testing of hydroplanes on Windermere and prevent the construction of a factory at Cockshott Point (below) to build more planes. She began a letter-writing campaign and took up a petition, protesting about the 'danger, turmoil and possible pecuniary damage' posed by the planes as well as the noise they caused which 'resembles millions of blue-bottles, plus a steam threshing engine'. 'It seems deplorable that this beautiful lake should be turned into another Brooklands or Hendon,' she wrote to *Country Life* magazine. 'A more inappropriate place for experimenting with flying machines could scarcely be chosen.'

With a parallel campaign staged by Hardwicke Rawnsley, then secretary of the National Trust, the protesters were successful in getting a public inquiry opened. Within months, plans for the factory had been abandoned and the hydroplanes disappeared from the lake. Fifteen years later, Beatrix was again involved in another campaign to save Cockshott Point, but this time working hand in hand with the National Trust.

Established by Robert Baden-Powell's sister Agnes in 1910, the movement encouraged resourcefulness, courage and loyalty; and learning outdoor skills formed an important part of members' development. 'It is a real pleasure to me to see young people enjoying the land that I love so well; though I cannot manage to enjoy every square yard of it myself,' she once wrote to a Guide leader. 'I feel as though the beauty of my own woods and fields might have been a bit wasted if it had not been useful to appreciative campers and holiday makers.'

National Trust Stalwart

Throughout her time as a Lake District resident, Beatrix maintained a close relationship with the National Trust. Although she didn't always agree with local decisions, she shared its ideals and supported its work in the area.

Supporter

With Beatrix's growing involvement in the Lake District, and her strong belief in the need to preserve its beauty and its traditions, it was almost inevitable that she would develop a relationship with the National Trust, co-established by her friend and mentor Hardwicke Rawnsley in 1895.

Bridge House

She kept the charity's then secretary Samuel Hamer informed of her work at Troutbeck Park Farm and her intention to leave it to the Trust in her will. She also tipped him off, in 1926, about the fact that Ambleside's iconic Bridge House might soon be up for sale. It 'attracts more curiosity from visitors than it altogether deserves,' she wrote, but realised 'it will be looked for, & missed, if it goes down'. She added that the 'sentiment of the town would be for preserving it' and, in a slightly dictatorial tone that would become less gentle in later correspondence, suggested Hamer 'make some inquiry before the sale planning matures'.

The Trust *did* act, and the funny little building spanning Stock Ghyll remains, to this day, a much-loved feature of Ambleside.

Cockshott Point

In 1927, she became more actively involved in a National Trust campaign to purchase a strip of land along Windermere's eastern shore. Cockshott Point (opposite) was again at risk, this time from 'disfigurement by extensive building and town extension', so she approached her fans in the USA for help in raising money. Wealthy Americans jumped at the chance to purchase one of the original, signed drawings of Peter Rabbit she sent out across the Atlantic, and she was soon able to let them know the appeal had been a success and that a 'dry gravel path is being made near the bank of the lake'. The National Trust still cares for the tranquil little promontory overlooking Belle Isle, and it remains a popular spot for holiday-makers and locals alike to enjoy a gentle lakeside stroll.

'I'm sure I am doing good in trying to save anything I can of our Lake country from being vulgarized; for, as true education advances, the beauty of unspoilt nature will be appreciated; and it would be a pity if the appreciation came too late. We do not wish to interfere with house building in suitable places, but we wish to preserve some portions of wild land unspoilt for the general good ...'

Monk Coniston Estate

In 1929, Beatrix's relationship with the National Trust changed beyond all recognition when a huge Lake District estate came up for sale. Stretching north from the head of Coniston Water all the way to Little Langdale and taking in Tilberthwaite too, the Monk Coniston estate included about a dozen farms, several cottages and quarries as well as Tarn Hows and fell land rising to 801m: almost 1,600 hectares (4,000 acres) in total.

Beatrix and the Trust were united in their desire to save this vast tract of land from being spoilt, particularly from 'building development creeping up from Skelwith Bridge' and the threat of afforestation posed by the Forestry Commission.

Family ties
Beatrix had a personal interest too: her great-grandfather Abraham Crompton had farmed at Holme Ground, Tilberthwaite, which was part of the estate. 'I have always longed to buy it back and give it to the Trust in remembrance,' she wrote to a friend. 'I was very much attached to my grandmother Jessy Crompton and said to be very like her, "only not so good looking!!!" according to old folks.'

Business head
Sentimentality may have played a role in the purchase, but the astute Mrs Heelis didn't allow it to influence her business decisions. With her husband William carefully handling the legal side of things, she bought the entire estate. She kept half for herself and then sold the other half to the Trust once it had raised the necessary funds, all the while ensuring she didn't lose out in any way. 'I got back three quarters of the original purchase money of Monk Coniston while I kept the more valuable half of the estate,' she wrote to the National Trust's northern area representative Bruce Thompson in 1932. 'As I took the initial risk I was entitled to reap any advantage.'

Recognising Beatrix's skills as a land manager, the Trust asked her to look after their half of the property as well as her own. Now in her mid-sixties, she was taking on a new and demanding role, but one which allowed her to make her mark on large sections of the Lake District. It was a request she eagerly accepted, describing her new role as 'interesting work at other people's expense'. It was also a 'mark of confidence' that, she said, 'gratified me very much'.

'It seems that we have done a big thing; without premeditation; suddenly; inevitably – what else could one do? It will be a happy consummation if the Trust is able to turn this quixotic venture into a splendid reality.'

Opposite Tarn Hows

A new job

At an age when most people's thoughts are turning to retirement or at least a slower pace of life, Beatrix – now 64 – was refurbishing cottages, negotiating property boundaries, interviewing potential tenants, overseeing the repair of walls, fences, footpaths and drains, managing woodland, and carrying out all sorts of improvements across the Monk Coniston estate.

She even oversaw what went into some of the old farmhouses, indulging in her zeal for buying oak furniture at sales and auctions. Where did she find the energy for such detail while also managing so many properties and farming in her own right? Of course, she had William's help, but, even working as a pair, what they managed to achieve was impressive.

One of her most difficult relationships was with the recently appointed sanitary inspector whose job it was to inspect homes and decide whether or not they were fit for habitation. Although she was keen to modernise properties, she wanted to ensure the work respected the traditional architecture, and the official's often arbitrary rules made this tricky. He saw overcrowding as an important issue too, but Beatrix wasn't about to turn families out on to the streets during hard times. 'If the sanitary inspector got to the Castle there might be words,' she wrote to Samuel Hamer about the tiny Rose Castle cottage at Tarn Hows. 'Talk of overcrowding in a slum! There are 8 beds in a small chamber ... with one narrow window.'

Bruce Thompson

After many years of carefully nurturing the estate on behalf of the National Trust, it's hardly surprising that, when it was able to appoint a full-time land agent in 1936, Beatrix should have some reservations.

Bruce Thompson ended up having a long and successful career with the Trust in the Lake District, and was popular with most people he dealt with, but his relationship with Beatrix was always a challenging one. Her letters to him are full of information and advice, sometimes with a slightly interfering tone. On some occasions, he took her advice; on others, he didn't. And when he didn't, she took it to the highest level. 'He seems to have no sense at all,' she wrote in 1939 to Donald Matheson, assistant secretary to the National Trust. Not holding anything back, she described him as 'too deficient in experience and taste' and having 'no capacity for dealing with tradesmen'.

Left Shepherd rounding up sheep near Loweswater, 1930s

Above Beatrix in her sixties with her favourite shepherd Tom Storey (see page 26)

Lasting Legacy

Beatrix Heelis, née Potter, died just before Christmas 1943, aged 77, but her remarkable story didn't end there.

Thanks to her exceptional bequest to the National Trust, large areas of the Lake District have been protected from development. Her legacy lives on through the Trust and will continue to do so for generations to come.

An end – and a beginning

With her husband by her side, Beatrix died at Castle Cottage on 22 December 1943. She'd been ill for a while, struggling with bronchitis and a weak heart. With Tom Storey his only companion, William scattered her ashes, as she had requested, in the hills above Sawrey. He outlived her by less than two years; Tom then took William's ashes to the same spot. The exact location will never be known: the last custodian of the secret, Tom's son Geoff, having taken it to his grave.

Above The last known photograph of Beatrix Potter

National Trust
In a letter of condolence to her husband the day after her death, National Trust secretary Donald Matheson described Beatrix as a 'many-sided genius' who 'demonstrated her understanding of the problems of preservation in the Lake District and how they were linked to those of successful sheep farming'.

Her death opened a new chapter in the history of the Trust – indeed in the history of the Lake District. As a grieving William struggled with the unenviable task of settling and distributing her estate, the conservation charity was able to announce, in February 1944, its 'greatest ever Lakeland gift'. She had left it 15 farms, covering more than 1,600 hectares (4,000 acres) of land, and numerous cottages and houses. Upon his death in 1945, William also left properties to the Trust, including his office in Hawskhead.

Cottage tenant

When the tenancy of Castle Cottage became available in 2011, tour guide Mandy Marshall and her husband Bill jumped at the chance to live in Beatrix Potter's former home. The couple had moved to Cumbria a couple of years earlier and, as Mandy explains, saw this as a 'unique opportunity' to live in an historic property that would never become available to buy.

Beatrix specified in her will that her houses were to be let to reliable tenants, so it's hardly surprising the Marshalls, and other prospective tenants, underwent a lengthy interview with the National Trust before moving into the five-bedroom property.

The house was renovated just before Mandy and Bill moved in, and the National Trust continues to maintain the property sensitively. In 2015, the walled garden was rebuilt with the help of old photographs.

Above Moss Eccles Tarn is just a short walk from Hill Top and Castle Cottage. Beatrix and her husband William enjoyed boating and fishing here on summer evenings

Left The Beatrix Potter Gallery in Hawkshead

Living memorials

Hill Top

As requested by William, Hill Top was to remain a tribute to Beatrix's life, with her furniture and other belongings – much of it moved from Castle Cottage and Troutbeck Park Farm – on display for visitors to see. The National Trust opened the house to the public in 1946, and since then it has been a place of pilgrimage for Beatrix Potter fans from around the world. From the oak longcase clock featured in *The Tailor of Gloucester* to the dolls, trinkets and mementoes crowding the rooms upstairs, Hill Top provides a snapshot of the life of a remarkable woman.

Cottages

While Hill Top exists as a museum, most of Beatrix's other properties provide homes and, in the case of the farms, livelihoods for 21st-century families. Her will stipulates that her houses and cottages, ranging from tiny farm workers' cottages to the grand Georgian mansion of Belmount on the edge of Hawkshead, should be let rather than sold. If it weren't for these properties, it is easy to envisage some villages within the National Park becoming home only to tourists and those visiting their holiday homes – the pressure on the homes-to-rent market really is that intense.

Above The cottage at Hill Top as seen from its small kitchen garden

Left The Entrance Hall at Hill Top

Right View from one of the rooms at Hill Top

Farms

Beatrix was keen that farming traditions were kept going 'so far as possible' on her properties after her death. She wanted the landlord's sheep stocks on her fell farms to be maintained as 'pure Herdwick breed', and the National Trust today insists tenants on its relevant properties run a flock of these native sheep. The practices of dry-stone walling, coppicing and other age-old skills carry on much as they have done for centuries, while buildings are maintained and improved in ways that are in keeping with the age and style of the property – a practice that Beatrix herself initiated on behalf of the Trust when she managed Monk Coniston.

The Armitt

Beatrix was one of the early members of the Armitt Library, established as a subscription library in Ambleside in 1909. Its founders and supporters encouraged the study of Lakeland culture and natural history. During her lifetime, Beatrix donated books from her late father Rupert's library as well as a collection of her own archaeological drawings. When she died, she left the library hundreds of her own fungi watercolours and microscope studies. The Armitt is now an independent museum that is open to the public, and many of Beatrix's studies are on display there.

On the farm

Hill farmer Jon Watson is a convert to Herdwicks. When he moved to Yew Tree Farm on the Monk Coniston estate from North Yorkshire in 2002, he wasn't convinced of their worth.

He felt other breeds might be more profitable, and said as much to a visiting group of Beatrix Potter fans. The next year, the group returned for another visit. By then, all the sheep on Jon's farm were Herdwicks. 'Last year you claimed they were rubbish,' one of the members reminded him. 'Last year,' he replied, 'I hadn't tasted them.'

Businessman
Jon sells all his meat direct: none of his Herdwicks or belted Galloway cattle goes through the livestock auctions. He started Yew Tree Farm Heritage Meats in 2003 because he felt the distinctive Herdwick taste was being lost as farmers, instead of allowing the animals to mature naturally, were fattening lambs on expensive artificial concentrates. The meat was then entering the food chain as generic lamb. 'I decided to keep them over another year, let them graze naturally,' Jon explains. 'I end up with a dark, strong-flavoured meat that I can sell all year round at a better premium.'

Hill farming is not a lucrative business, so Jon is always thinking ahead, predicting what the markets will do. 'I'm not frightened of thinking outside the box and making changes,' he says.

'You've got to move not with the times, but *before* them.' Jon was the first farmer in the area to bring native cattle back to the fells. 'Some people laughed at us when we got the belted Galloways, but quite a few have since bought them off me.'

Farm Business Tenancies
Jon had to put forward a detailed business plan before he could be considered for the Yew Tree tenancy. While private farm tenancies, if they aren't passed from one generation to another, generally go to the highest bidder, the National Trust ensures it gets the right person for the property, judging them on their farm management skills and plans for the future. Such Farm Business Tenancies are often the only way into farming for people who are not going to take on a family farm.

The actor and the turkey
Half of Jon's farmhouse, used as Beatrix's home in the 2006 film *Miss Potter*, is let to holidaymakers. One of its more famous guests was actor Emma Thompson, who recently wrote three new Peter Rabbit stories for Beatrix Potter publisher Frederick Warne. One of these – *The Christmas Tale of Peter Rabbit* – features William, the turkey that can usually be seen strutting around Jon's yard.

Opposite Farmer Jon Watson with his flock of Herdwicks at Yew Tree Farm

Beatrix Potter's Lake District Today

The Lake District National Park came into being in 1951, eight years after Beatrix Potter's death, establishing statutory protection for the spectacular landscape and cultural heritage that this most forward-thinking of women so adored. Today, the National Trust manages about 20 per cent of the National Park, including huge expanses of the high fells, more than 90 tenanted farms and dozens of listed buildings. It owns the bed of England's deepest lake, Wastwater, and the summit of her highest mountain, Scafell Pike.

This guardianship has been made possible thanks, in part, to the bequest of Beatrix Potter and other landowners, but also to the generous donations of ordinary members of the public. As the UK's largest conservation charity, the Trust relies on membership subscriptions, gifts, legacies and the contribution made by thousands of volunteers. If you would like to help it continue its work in the 21st century and beyond, visit www.nationaltrust.org.uk to find out more about donating, visiting and volunteering.

Right Walkers on the Scafell path with Wastwater in the distance